THE STORY OF

ASTRONOMY

CAROLE STOTT

Illustrated by
CHRIS FORSEY

Troll Associates

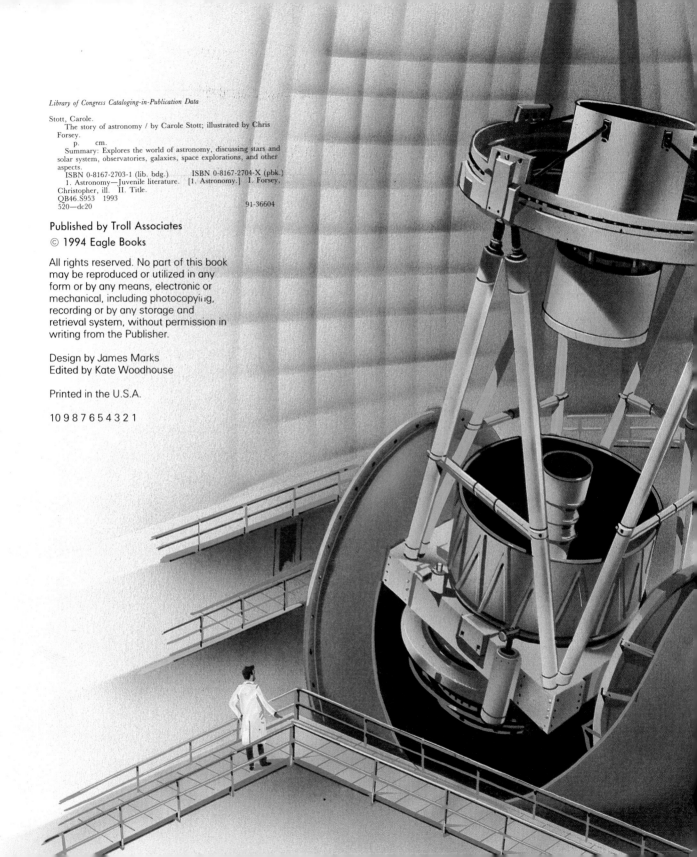

Library of Congress Cataloging-in-Publication Data

Stott, Carole.
   The story of astronomy / by Carole Stott; illustrated by Chris
Forsey.
      p.   cm.
   Summary: Explores the world of astronomy, discussing stars and
solar system, observatories, galaxies, space explorations, and other
aspects.
   ISBN 0-8167-2703-1 (lib. bdg.)   ISBN 0-8167-2704-X (pbk.)
   1. Astronomy—Juvenile literature.   [1. Astronomy.]   I. Forsey,
Christopher, ill.   II. Title.
QB46.S953   1993
520—dc20   91-36604

Published by Troll Associates

© 1994 Eagle Books

Design by James Marks
Edited by Kate Woodhouse

Printed in the U.S.A.

10 9 8 7 6 5 4 3 2 1

Contents

Watching the sky

The first humans were as fascinated by the sky as we are today. In the daytime they saw the sun and at night they watched the stars. Their day started when the sun rose into the sky and ended as it disappeared.

Later peoples realized that the sun also measured out a longer passage of time. In one year, made up of 365.25 days, the changing height of the sun in the sky produced the seasons: spring, summer, autumn, and winter. The moon appeared to change shape gradually from a new moon to a crescent to a full moon and back again. This happened approximately every 29.5 days and became their month.

▶ From early times, people have imagined patterns in the stars and used these patterns, or constellations, to guide them. They noticed five bright "stars" that moved. These were the planets Mercury, Venus, Mars, Jupiter, and Saturn.

Sun
Venus
Mercury
Saturn
Earth
Moon
Mars
Jupiter

▲ The ancient Greeks believed the Earth was the center of the universe with the planets orbiting it.

The sun at the center

In the 16th century, people started to explore Earth's surface. They quickly discovered that Earth was round, not flat as many people believed. At the same time people were discovering more about space.

In 1609, the recently invented telescope was used by the Italian astronomer, Galileo Galilei, to take a closer look at the sky. He was the first to see mountains on the moon, and he discovered that the night sky contains thousands more stars than we can see using our naked eyes alone.

Everything that Galileo saw made him, and others, believe that Earth could not be the central object in space. They realized that the theory published by the Polish astronomer, Copernicus, was right: Earth, its moon, and the planets all travel around the sun. The sun is at the center of its system of planets, the solar system. And the solar system is surrounded by millions and millions of stars. Together, they all make up the universe.

▶ Galileo spent a great deal of time observing the skies. He discovered four of the planet Jupiter's 16 moons. They travel around Jupiter, just as our moon travels around Earth.

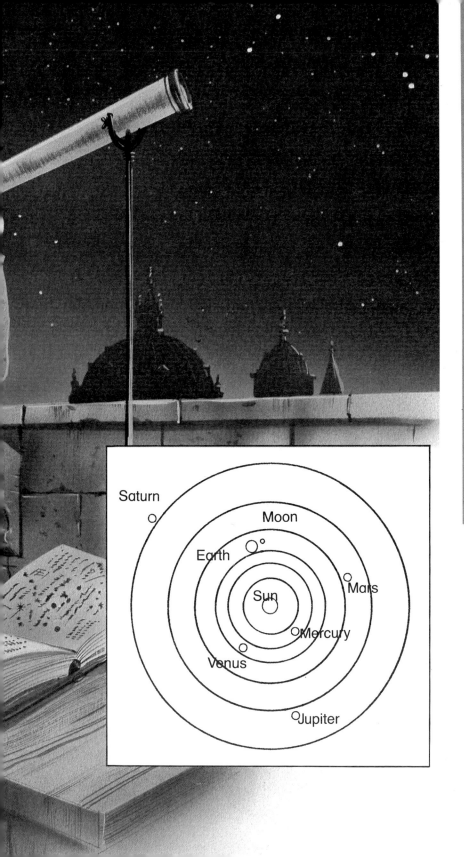

Saturn

Moon

Earth

Mars

Sun

Mercury

Venus

Jupiter

▲ Nicolaus Copernicus only dared to publish his theory of the universe in 1543 when he was dying. He was right to be afraid, as people were later burned at the stake for supporting his idea that Earth was not the center of the universe.

◄ Copernicus is remembered as the astronomer who laid the foundations of our modern view of the universe. His theory was that the planets, including Earth, all revolved around the sun.

7

The solar system

Earth and eight other planets travel around the sun. These planets, their moons, rocky bodies called asteroids, and wandering comets are all part of the solar system. As long as records have been kept, people have known of Mercury, Venus, Earth, Mars, Jupiter, and Saturn. The first four are rock planets. Jupiter and Saturn are largely gas.

The three most distant planets, Uranus, Neptune, and Pluto, were all discovered within the last 220 years. William Herschel discovered Uranus in 1781. He observed it unexpectedly from his garden in England using a homemade telescope.

Later, astronomers discovered that Uranus did not travel around the sun in the way they expected; they thought the attraction of another planet must be pulling it. That planet, Neptune, was identified in 1846 by the German astronomers, Johann Galle and Heinrich d'Arrest. The same process led to the discovery of the last planet, Pluto, in 1930.

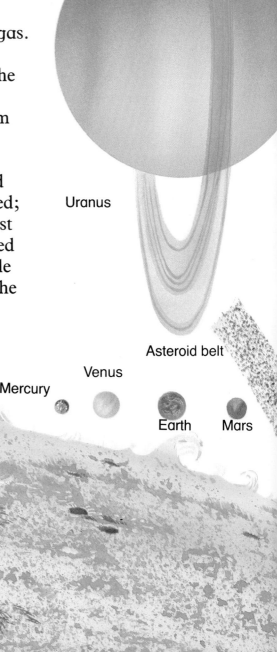

Uranus

Asteroid belt

Venus

Mercury

Earth   Mars

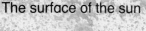
The surface of the sun

Neptune

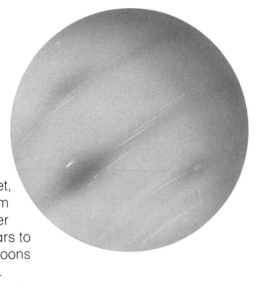

Each of the sun's planets has individual qualities. For example, Uranus is a giant planet, surrounded by a system of rings. Unlike the other major planets, it appears to lie on its side with its moons orbiting its mid-section.

The asteroid belt is made up of thousands of small planets, most of which lie between Mars and Jupiter.

▲ William Herschel, a musician and amateur astronomer who discovered Uranus.

Pluto

▲ Pluto was detected on photographs by the American, Clyde Tombaugh, in 1930.

Jupiter

Saturn

Uranus

Neptune

Pluto

The southern sky

As European explorers traveled farther south, they saw new stars in the night sky. They watched the stars from their ships, but to plot the stars' positions they set up their telescopes on firm land. When they returned home, they brought their newly created maps of the southern sky with them.

Three thousand years earlier, Greek observers of the northern sky had already grouped the stars into constellations. Around the stars they drew pictures of people and animals from their myths and folk stories. In the 17th century, people formed the newly discovered southern stars into constellation patterns, too.

The explorers also saw two fuzzy patches of light. We now know they are collections of millions and millions of stars. They are called the Large and Small Magellanic Clouds, after Ferdinand Magellan, the Portuguese explorer.

▶ The explorers and map makers chose patterns for the southern skies to represent creatures of the southern lands, such as the peacock, toucan, and flying fish.

Observatories

Astronomers observe the sky, and the place they work is called an observatory. It can be very large or very small. The largest observatories are specially designed buildings with domed roofs. They contain the most powerful telescopes in the world. These observatories may be owned by universities or one or more countries.

A number of important observatories were built in Europe in the 17th century, soon after the invention of the telescope. The first big American observatories were built in the late 19th century.

When an observatory is built today, it is placed well away from city lights, which make the sky too bright for good observing. An observatory is usually built on top of a mountain, high above Earth's pollution, so the astronomer can look at a clear sky. But the best observing is done out in space, away from Earth altogether. The Hubble Space Telescope is a space observatory now orbiting Earth. It sends pictures back to astronomers on Earth.

▶ The Anglo-Australian Telescope (AAT) in Australia is one of the best telescopes in the world. It has been used to study objects at great distances, such as quasars and galaxies, as well as the sun's nearest neighbors, like Venus.

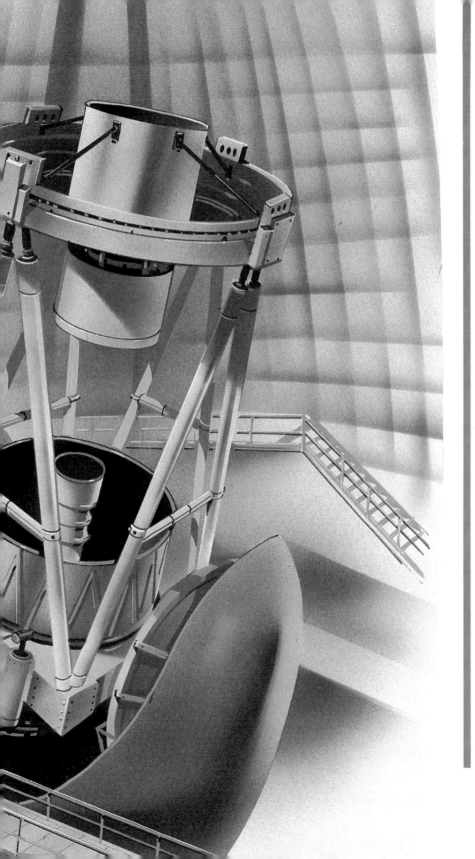

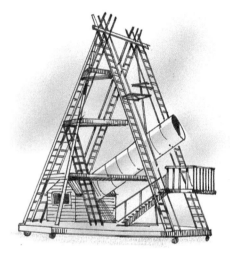

▲ Herschel used this telescope to discover two of Saturn's satellites in 1789.

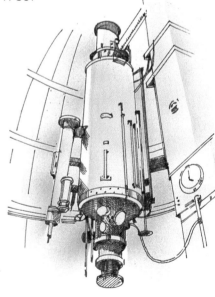

▲ The Lowell telescope in the United States was built at the end of the 19th century. Percival Lowell used it to observe Mars.

Keeping records

Astronomers keep diaries of their observations, describing what they see. The first astronomers made pencil or ink drawings. Today, photographs and computers make better records.

When cameras were developed in the 19th century, astronomers soon turned them toward the heavens. At first they photographed the moon and the sun, but later they were able to take pictures of stars and planets.

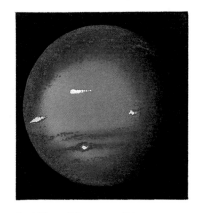

▲ When Voyager 2 recorded this view of Neptune, it was 2,925,000 miles (4,680,000 kilometers) from Earth. The image shows the haze that covers the planet. The red is sunlight on the haze.

◄ Voyager 2 was launched in 1977. It is a four-planet probe that passed Jupiter in 1979, Saturn in 1981, Uranus in 1986, and Neptune in 1989. It sent a vast amount of fascinating, new information back to Earth.

Photographs give astronomers permanent records. They can study them whenever they like, noticing things that others have missed. Stars, galaxies, comets, moons, and even a planet, Pluto, have all been discovered in photographs.

Today, sophisticated cameras and computers are used to record and analyze information. Television cameras are sent into space to record views that are impossible to photograph from Earth. Pictures revealed Mercury's craters and Mars' rocky terrain. We have seen Saturn's rings and the distant, icy worlds of Uranus and Neptune close up. Other cameras point into deep space and record other groups of stars called galaxies.

The life of a star

Astronomers were first interested in finding the positions of the stars. In the 19th century they started to learn what stars are made of. They discovered that even though stars are all balls of hot gas, there are many different types and sizes.

Astronomers came to realize that stars have a life cycle, just as humans do. Like people, stars are born, live, grow older, and eventually die. But stars live for millions of years, and so change very slowly compared with humans.

▶ A star begins as a cloud of material. Gradually, the cloud condenses, the temperature rises, and a star cluster forms. The star cluster is loosely bound and slowly breaks up. A star like the sun then settles down for about 10,000 million years, giving off energy. When the energy runs out, the sun will shrink and become a white dwarf star.

▲ It is rare to see a star change. One chance is when a star suddenly explodes and dies. The star, called a supernova at this stage, becomes much brighter. Then gradually it dims, until it is lost from view.

Stars are born together in groups from spinning clouds of gas and dust. As they get older, they move away from each other. Our closest star, the sun, is now a middle-aged star and will live for another 5 billion years.

Galaxies

The sun belongs to a large family of more than 100 billion stars called the Milky Way Galaxy. The Milky Way is disk-shaped with a central bulge, with many old stars towards the center, and fewer, younger stars at its edges.

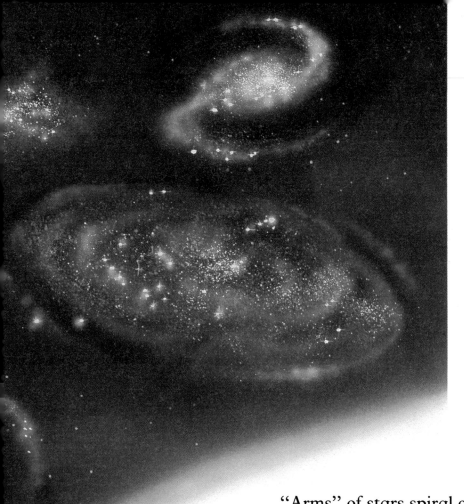

▲ In the 1920s, the American astronomer, Edwin Hubble, showed that there are other star systems like our galaxy.

◀ Astronomers observe galaxies millions and millions of miles away. They are able to plot their paths and to see how they have developed.

"Arms" of stars spiral out from the center of the Milky Way, so some people describe it as a giant pinwheel. The sun is in one of these arms, about two-thirds of the way from the center.

A hundred years ago, astronomers thought that the Milky Way was the only galaxy in the universe. Now they know that there are many more galaxies of different shapes. Some, like ours, have arms of stars. Others are ball-shaped and some have no regular shape at all. We also know that not only do these galaxies spin, they are also all rushing away from each other. So the universe is getting bigger and bigger all the time.

The start of the universe

◄ Astronomers study the material, size, distance, and movement of objects in the universe. In this way they calculate the age of the universe and understand how it has developed.

At the beginning of time, all the material in the universe was crammed into one spot. Scientists think a massive explosion about 15 billion years ago, called the big bang, made the universe start to expand. The material gradually formed into galaxies and stars. Our sun was born and, about 4.6 billion years ago, Earth and the other solar-system planets were formed out of the leftover material surrounding the sun.

Astronomers would like to know what the future holds. They believe that the universe could continue getting bigger as the galaxies rush away from each other. Or the galaxies may slow down, stop, and move back to where they came from, colliding in a big crunch. The universe would then be a single lump and the whole process might start again.

▲ This experiment shows how the universe is expanding. As the balloon expands, the dots, which represent the galaxies in the universe, all move away from each other.

21

Messages from space

Astronomers have always used their eyes to investigate the universe. But, over the last 60 years, they have developed other ways of learning about space.

Radio and other types of waves can be received from regions in space that look empty. So we know there is more in the universe than we can see. Two of the most puzzling types of astronomical objects were discovered by radio astronomy. Quasars were identified in 1963. Astronomers know little about them, except that they are distant starlike objects. Pulsars, which are the spinning remains of massive stars, were first discovered in 1967. The fastest known pulsar is the Crab, which spins every 0.033 seconds.

◀ These radio telescopes are part of the Very Large Array in New Mexico. There are 27 dishes, each 81 feet (25 meters) in diameter, which combine as if they were a radio telescope of 23 miles (34 kilometers) across.

▲ This radio-telescope picture shows the center of our galaxy. The strongest radio signals are red, and the weakest are blue. An ordinary telescope could not produce an image like this; it would only show the stars nearer to us.

23

Exploring the moon

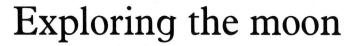

The moon is the closest body to Earth. For
hundreds of years people dreamed of traveling
there. But they had to wait until the large rockets
and spacecraft needed for traveling in space were
developed. It was on July 21, 1969 that Neil
Armstrong became the first man to set foot on
the moon.

In the 1970s other astronauts set up experiments on the moon that worked for up to five years after they left. One experiment measured shock waves like those felt on Earth from earthquakes. Reflectors on the moon can still be used today to bounce laser beams back to Earth. These help scientists to measure the distance between Earth and the moon to within a few inches.

◄ In the early 1970s, special moon buggies, called lunar rovers, carried the astronauts and their equipment across the moon. Astronauts have traveled over 55 miles (90 kilometers) of the moon's surface.

▲ The Russians landed Lunokhods on the moon, one in 1970 and a second in 1973. These robot explorers sent back over 100,000 pictures of the moon to Earth.

Spacecraft

Astronomers can take a closer look at their surroundings by sending equipment into space. The "space age" began in 1957 when the former Soviet Union launched Sputnik 1, the first artificial satellite to orbit Earth. In 1961, Yuri Gagarin became the first person to travel into space.

Since then, American space probes have been sent to investigate all the planets in the solar system, except Pluto. The European Giotto space probe investigated Halley's Comet and photographed our first close-up views of a comet. Many satellites with scientific equipment have been launched to orbit Earth and record information from a variety of space objects.

▼ These satellites are all performing different tasks.
1 Hubble space telescope
2 Skylab space station
3 Infra-red astronomy satellite
4 LANDSAT for mapping Earth from space
5 SARSAT rescue satellite

1

2

The future

The Magellan space probe is now orbiting Venus. The Galileo probe is traveling to Jupiter, where it will make a two-year study of the planet and its moons. The Cassini mission, to study Saturn and its rings over a three-year period, is being planned. Spacecraft can take many years to design and build, and the distances they travel are so vast that astronomers have to wait patiently for years for the results.

In the next century astronauts may return to the moon to set up a base or even travel farther and go to Mars. There will always be more to learn and discover. The search for greater understanding of the universe is neverending.

▶ Space scientists are preparing a new space station. Once it is in orbit around Earth, they plan to use it as a home and an office from where they can continue their exploration of space.

Fact file

The sun
The sun is almost 870,000 miles (1.4 million kilometers) in diameter. This is 109 times greater than Earth's diameter. The sun is about 300,000 times heavier than Earth.

Moonlight
The moon has no light of its own. It shines because it reflects light from the sun. The portion of the moon's lit surface that is visible from Earth shows the phase of the moon.

▲ The only star usually visible in the daytime is the sun. When there is an eclipse of the sun, the moon stops the sun's light from reaching Earth. For a very short time daylight disappears and the sky becomes dark enough to show up other stars.

The moon
Anyone with reasonable eyesight can look at the moon and see dark and light patches. Early observers thought the light areas were water and called them *mare*, which means sea. We know there is no water on the moon but we still use the original description.

The red planet
Mars is sometimes called the "red planet." The red color comes from Mars' soil and rocks. Strong winds cause dust storms, which blow the red soil across Mars' surface.

Voyager 1 and Voyager 2

Voyager 1 and Voyager 2 were launched in 1977. They have studied Jupiter, Saturn, Uranus, Neptune, and many of their moons. Each spacecraft carries computers and video cameras, as well as other scientific instruments, but each weighs less than a small car.

The Milky Way

Our galaxy is called the Milky Way. At night it appears as a hazy river of milky light across the dark sky. The light comes from the 100,000 million stars the galaxy contains.

Women in space

The first woman in space was the Russian cosmonaut Valentina Tereshkova in June 1963. Sally Ride was the first woman astronaut from the United States to fly into space. She traveled aboard the Space Shuttle Challenger in June 1983. Helen Sharman became the first Briton in space when she flew to the Russian Mir space station in May 1991.

Satellites

Seven of the nine planets in the solar system have satellites, also known as moons, orbiting them. Human-made satellites are space instruments that orbit Earth, many as much as 22,300 miles (36,000 kilometers) away, but others at only a few hundred miles above its surface. Some satellites look into deep space, others look down to Earth.

▲ Many scientists believe that a huge comet or an asteroid collided with Earth around 64 million years ago. They believe that the drastic effect it had on the climate of the Earth may have resulted in the death of dinosaurs.

Index